The Ultimate Handbook for Women to Manifest Love and Attract Men

A Secret Guide to Enhance Your Feminine Allure and Get the Man of Your Dreams

DANIEL MONETIER

the suggested remedies, techniques, or information in this book.

Upon using the contents and information contained in this book, you agree to hold harmless the Author from and against any damages, costs, and expenses, including any legal fees potentially resulting from the application of any of the information provided by this book. This disclaimer applies to any loss, damages or injury caused by the use and application, whether directly or indirectly, of any advice or information presented, whether for breach of contract, tort, negligence, personal injury, criminal intent, or under any other cause of action.

You agree to accept all risks of using the information presented inside this book.

You agree that by continuing to read this book, where appropriate and/or necessary, you shall consult a professional (including but not limited to your doctor, attorney, or financial advisor or such other advisor as needed) before using any of the suggested remedies, techniques, or information in this book.

Table of Contents

Introduction

When you are in your 30s and you still haven't found the man of your dreams, maybe there is something wrong about how you deal with men. If you have a hard time talking to men, try to assess yourself. Why is it that until today, you find it hard to deal with men with grace and confidence? That no matter how much you convince yourself that it's completely fine to mingle with them, still you can't find the courage to do it. When you aren't that confident about the way you look, you tend to keep yourself away from attractive men. That is why most of the time, you are just content of seeing them from afar – and not making any move to get closer to them. Even though you want to act as natural as possible around men, you still end up being awkward whenever you're with them. The worst part is, you are even afraid of taking the first step to getting to know them more. Aren't you tired of being alone? Why do you let this happen?

In this book, I am going to teach you how to achieve your main goal – to attract the man of your dreams. I will present to you some practical solutions and tips to get them hooked on you and consider you their better half. I will help you transform from a woman who lacks self-confidence to a woman with robust confidence in less than 30 days. I know how hard it is to deal with men especially how to know and understand the things they like in a woman. If you have experienced rejection from different kinds of men before, let me help you stand again. I will show you the ways on how to overcome that fear of rejection for good. I will teach you how to be strong and be able to deal with men more effectively next time.

Hi, my name is Daniel Monetier. I am a life dating coach who helps couples keep their relationship strong and rekindle the love and spark they have for each other. I have been counseling women how to attract the man of their dreams by revealing to them what men truly want in a woman. I also help women know and understand many different men's behaviors and how they handle relationships with a woman. I hope this book will truly help you exude that much-needed confidence around men. I also wish you will find the man of your dreams the soonest time possible.

Imagine how sweet life can be if you finally find the man of your dreams. Life can get even sweeter when the man you love finally asks you to marry him and start building a family together. The truth is you can find many kinds of men in any kind of setting such as in the workplace. Never lose hope. One day, you will be able to find the right man and start building dreams together. You just have to trust yourself that you can do it and be able to develop that confidence to handle situations effectively.

One friendly advice though, get the man whom you truly want. Choose the one who will be most suited for you. Most importantly, have that bulletproof, social confidence that will make men draw near to you and chase you anytime, anywhere. If you know how to attract men properly, you don't need to use speed-dating apps such as Tinder anymore. When you know how to deal with men and make them fall for you, that could be your biggest advantage.

The different sets of information written in this book are proven true and effective. Many women have been thanking me for all the tips I've imparted them. They are so grateful for all the things I've shared with them and how these changed their perspective of men. These also helped them build deeper connections and meaningful relationships with the man they are interested in.

What I will be unveiling in this book is the same technique I shared with them. This step by step technique is easy to follow and provides effective results. My expertise on this subject can help you be equipped with the necessary skills and knowledge for you take dating game on a whole new level. The knowledge you will learn from this book will guide you in maintaining a good relationship with the man you love. This will also help increase the levels of intimacy and commitment in your relationship. When a man gets a sufficient amount of attention and love from you, he will never cheat on you. That is another thing I'd like to teach you in this book.

I certainly know how hard it is to find and keep the man you've been longing for. The process can be so hard, but you can always take the shortcut. The truth is, it is so expensive to hire a life dating coach just to help you find the man of your dreams. I have many clients who are paying me lots of money for different dating advice and tips. But I will not let you pay for my services. I am offering help for free! Why? Because I simply want to help women who have low self-esteem and make them more confident around men. I want them to find that one man who will fulfill their dreams and longings.

Remember, you are a woman, and you deserve the best man in the world! I hope I can play a part in your journey towards finding that perfect man. If there's a man in your life right now that you really like, do everything to get him. Use this book as a guide in making him interested in you and fall in love with you.

The techniques written in this book are proven effective and yield incredible results for single women of all ages and looks. Each chapter of this book will teach you how to be more pleasing to men and make them chase you. Some chapters contain information on how to encourage men to pursue you and make them go madly in love with you. This book will also teach women with low self-confidence to start spreading their wings and show the world what they've got.

For over 5 years of studying relationships and men, I've found out that the physical attributes of a woman are not the sole basis for men to like her. That you don't need to be so pretty, intelligent, rich, or famous to get the man of your dreams. All you need to do is follow the techniques written in this book and constantly practice them. Sounds good to be true? Well, that's what hundreds of women I coached thought, too.

Start living your life on your terms and take the first step to attract any men you want. Grab a copy of this handbook now to unlock the necessary techniques in

making men fall in love with you and take your
dating life to the next level.

Chapter 1 – The 15 Qualities That Men Want in a Woman

A lot of women have a hard time finding the man of their dreams. This is because they have little knowledge about the different qualities that men are looking for in a woman. Men are naturally mysterious and less-expressive. It is hard to read their minds and oftentimes, they do things differently. Contrary to popular belief, men aren't just looking for the superficial beauty of a woman. More often than not, they look for something more valuable – like character, skills/talents, and the so-called inner beauty. Men can be polygamous by nature. But when they finally decide to settle down, they do everything to find their only forever queen. If you want to know the different qualities that men are looking for in a woman, continue reading below.

These are the 15 qualities that men want in a woman:

1. ***Intelligence***

    Women who can talk about anything at any given time can easily catch a man's attention. They are also more likely to find the finest guys in town. Being intelligent doesn't necessarily mean you have to graduate with

Latin honors, be like a walking encyclopedia, or possess an IQ close to Einstein's. You just need to equip yourself with enough knowledge and wisdom to share with men. To do this, read a lot of books and constantly update yourself with the latest information. One important tip, when you are talking with men, avoid sounding like a know-it-all kind of person. You can be smart but not cocky. Remember, a man will always try to protect his ego. If you insist to be more superior to him, he will get offended and turned off.

2. ***Sense of Humor***

A monotonous life is indeed a boring life! If you are used to living a boring life, you will find it hard to look for a potential partner. Most men prefer a woman who knows how to break the ice and is fun to be with. Since men can be tough at times, they need someone who will lighten their mood when they can't contain their emotions. A woman who will crack small jokes or make funny gestures just to make them feel good again. If you want to attract Mr. Right, smile more often and loosen up. But please avoid throwing personal and below-the-belt jokes to men. Having a good sense of humor should not give you a license to make fun of others. You can be funny without degrading someone's morale. Men don't like that!

3. ***Kindness***

This is one trait of a woman that men find so attractive. A kind-hearted woman is a genuine person. She is always willing to understand and considers the welfare of others. When a man tries to approach you, make sure to shower him with your kindness. It doesn't matter whether you like him or not – just be nice to him. Kind women are more likely to meet a man who can be their potential partner in life. It is important to note, however, that not all men are good – some will just take advantage of your kindness. When your instinct tells you that the guy is a creeper, do the initiative to run away.

4. ***Confidence***

We live in a society where men are expected to exude more confidence than women. A woman of confidence is sexy, fierce, and empowered. She is considered a gem by many hopeful men. A confident woman can be a man's powerful tool in building his dreams in the future. As a member of the female population, you are viewed by society as someone meek, submissive, and less confident. But you can be more than that. You are also entitled to have that confidence that will help you achieve all your dreams in life – including your dream guy. Be more confident when you're having a conversation with a man. Do it in a way that he will not get intimidated and irritated. When talking to guys, always maintain eye contact and establish that much-needed rapport. That could be a good start.

5. *Loyalty*

Loyal women are capable of handling and maintaining a good relationship. They can keep their promises until the very end. Men want their women to be always faithful to them – no matter what challenges they may face in the future. They always long for a loyal partner who will never cheat on them. A woman's loyalty is a man's most powerful weapon to stay in the relationship. If you think you are capable of staying faithful to your man, that could be your advantage.

6. *Honesty*

Honesty is the foundation of trust. Relationships that are built in honesty and trust are more likely to last. When a guy starts asking questions about your life, respond by telling only the truthful information and facts. You don't have to lie just to brag and impress the guy. Be honest in imparting important information about your life. You can keep the most important ones especially if you aren't ready yet to accept him in your world. Remember, that man can be your potential partner. He will soon find out if these pieces of information are true and valid.

7. *Trust*

    Trust is another important factor that makes a relationship last. It is the basis of a strong and healthy union between a man and a woman. Men don't like women who are insecure, doubtful, and paranoid. They hate it when you are always accusing them of something they didn't do. They're easily irritated when you keep on throwing them questions from time to time. If you want to catch the most perfect man on earth, start building a sense of trust. Develop that trust within yourself so that you can give it to other people. Bear in mind that men need someone they can trust with, and someone who can trust them in return.

8. *Maturity*

    Studies show that women mature quicker than men. Women analyze all the things and possibilities first before making a decision. They study almost every detail of the situation and make sure everything is set before giving it a go. These are signs of maturity – in which men are lacking sometimes. Men, on the other hand, can be playful, immature, and impulsive. They love to experience all the fun and adventure in this world. Most guys prefer a woman who is mature in making decisions in life. They need this kind of woman to build a sense of direction and be more responsible for everything they do. If you think you are a mature kind of woman, then you have higher chances to be recognized.

9. *Affection*

Men are less-affectionate and not showy. They do not want to show their vulnerability or weak sides. This may be related to the principle of machismo or the sense of being manly and self-reliant. Men have their own, special ways of expressing their love and affection to a woman. They do these in such a way that they will still look like yeah, a "real man!" Men sometimes show their love by simply saying "I Love You!", giving gifts, kisses/hugs, or introducing you to his friends and family. What's interesting about men is they love to receive so much attention and love gestures. They may not show it but the truth is, they are actually a sucker of intimacy. If you are willing to give your unconditional and endless love (and affection) to the man of your dreams, then do it! That will make him appreciate your presence more and go madly in love with you.

10. *Respect*

A woman who shows respect to herself and other people is taken seriously by men. Nowadays, casual sex and hookups are considered normal. It is much easier to look for a sexual partner than a lifetime companion. Most guys aren't that interested in women who just love partying and getting drunk. They still prefer women who live a simple and conservative kind of life. As a woman, you need to learn how to value yourself more and be able to know your worth. Avoid things that will make men take advantage of you. Also, avoid disrespectful men as well – they don't deserve you!

11. *Determination*

Men are typically looking for a woman who can be their future wife or life partner. When men are in a relationship with a woman, they study every aspect of her personality or character. If they see something that turns them off, they oftentimes lose the momentum. This is one of the reasons why most men suddenly disappear in a relationship – leaving the woman clueless about what exactly happened. Men prefer a woman who knows her goals in life. A woman who, despite having imperfections, is still willing to risk everything just to achieve her dreams and ambitions in life. Most importantly, a woman who will not easily give up no matter what adversities may come along the way. If you are the woman we are talking about, you are lucky and it would definitely be easier for you to find a lifetime partner.

12. *Commitment*

Commitment is one quality that takes a lot of time to achieve. When you commit in a relationship, you are offering your 100% self to your significant other. You are promising to devote most of your time and energy to that person. Men find it hard to commit to any kind of relationship especially during their younger years. Single men like to explore the world and maximize the time they have before getting into a more serious and steady kind of relationship. One of the reasons why they constantly get into and out of the relationship is because they want to finally meet "the one". They are searching for that woman who is willing to commit and give her 100% in the relationship. Just a tip, when you make a promise to a guy, do everything to fulfill that promise. That is one important sign of commitment.

13. ***Humility***

    People who always remain humble are the best kind of people. They radiate positive energies to those around them. A humble woman is compassionate – she always considers the welfare of others and sets aside her happiness. This quality makes a woman even more beautiful and lovable. Men like a woman who remains humble no matter what her achievements in life are.

14. ***Passion***

    A burning passion keeps the relationship stronger and more long-lasting. Passionate individuals are bold enough to show their intense emotions and motives. They are also persistent and goal-oriented. A passionate woman can fully satisfy the sexual needs of a man. She is intense and desirably sexy – one that can drive a man crazy. Be reminded that passion is not just about sex alone. Passion is also about the things you do and plan to do in life – your hobbies, skills, desires, ambitions, etc. When you have a dream that you badly want to achieve, you do everything just to get it. You do it with love and passion. Men like passionate women who can keep the love burning 'til the very end.

15. ***Decisiveness***

Decisiveness is defined as the ability to make firm decisions quickly and effectively. Being decisive does not mean you need to be arrogant, stubborn, or hasty. It simply means you can decide with speed and clarity during crucial times. When a man asks you about your decision or opinion, answer him right away. Do not give indefinite answers such as, "I have no idea.", "It's up to you!", or "You decide!" This will turn him off and may label you as clingy and indecisive. Men values a woman who knows how to make the right choices and decisions in life. They see that woman as strong-willed and independent – a kind of woman who can be a good wife in the future.

If you think you possess some or all these qualities, Congratulations! You are one step closer to your dream – getting the man of your dreams!

Chapter 2 – How to be Confident around Men

Being confident when dealing with men is key to finding the right man or a lifetime partner. When you dare to approach men with fewer inhibitions, you can fully immerse yourself into their world. The struggle of exuding confidence around men is constantly being faced by some women nowadays.

One of the reasons why women find it hard to be confident around men is they are afraid to be judged by society. They fear being labeled as a low-class woman who just wants to gain attention from the opposite sex. Another reason is self-doubt, which includes low self-esteem and self-acceptance. Some women find it hard to accept the way they look, their imperfections/shortcomings, their bad attitudes, etc. While it's a known fact that men always look for the physical attractiveness of a lady, it is important to note that men also consider the totality of a woman. Most men are looking for a woman who is more than just a pretty face. A kind of woman who also possesses a good heart and soul.

The 9 Physical Attributes that Men Find Attractive in a Woman

Men are a lover of physical beauty. They love to see beautiful and attractive women who can fulfill their fantasies. According to this study, when a man checks out a woman, he is making a reproductive fitness assessment. Men are obsessed with physically attractive women who can carry their genes someday. This is the reason why beautiful, sexy, and attractive women can easily find the man of their dreams.

So, what exactly are the physical features that attract men the most? Here's the list:

1. *Low Waist-to-Hip Ratio*
    - According to scientists, a waist-to-hip (WHR) ratio of 0.7 (7/10) is the most ideal WHR for women. This ratio is associated with women's general health and fertility. Men prefer women with low WHR because they typically have smaller waistlines and wider hips. They also believe that women with wider hips are perfect for childbearing. If you have an hourglass figure, men will surely find you. But if you don't, you can always try doing fitness training and exercise to achieve that body type.

2. *Glowing Skin*
   - Having a soft, smooth, and glowing skin is a sign of youth, good health, and better life choices. A woman with radiant skin knows how to take care of her body and present herself to the world. She also keeps herself away from harmful substances such as alcohol, cigarettes, or prohibited drugs. Men cannot resist a woman with naturally healthy and glowing skin. They find her more physically attractive and worthy. Also, different studies show that glowing skin is associated with good fertility and vitality.

3. *Long, Shiny Hair*
   - A woman's hair is her crowning glory. Men find women with long, shiny hair sexually attractive. They go crazy over women who keep their hair healthy and uncut. Healthy hair is a sign of a woman's good health and nutrition, personal hygiene and good grooming. This is also a major indication of extreme femininity, sexual health, and fertility.

4. *White and Bright Teeth*
   - White, bright, and healthy teeth symbolize good oral hygiene. No one can resist a person with excellently white and

sparkling teeth. Men are easily attracted to a woman with proper oral hygiene. A healthy oral cavity can create good conversations that can lead to romantic or intimate moments. It can also help you flash your best smile without any hesitation.

5. *Nice Eyes*
   - Men prefer a woman with a nice pair of large, round eyes. Women with big eyes are more expressive and appealing. Psychology explains that when a person is in love, his eyes are unconsciously dilating and becoming bigger. That may be the reason why people with larger eyes look happier and content. Another good reason why men prefer women with larger eyes is it makes them look hotter and sexier.

6. *Sexy Lips*
   - Men find it sexy and irresistible when a woman flashes her red, medium-sized, and kissable lips. Most people think that Angelina Jolie's thick, pouty lips are the ideal female lips that men adore. This may be true for some men who like to be showered by a million kisses for a day. But according to this research, men prefer

thin to medium-sized lips of a woman. If you are struggling to achieve that perfect luscious lips you've been wanting to achieve, you can always rely on the power of lipstick. Men will notice you when you wear red, glossy lipstick. One study of Manchester University found out that men can stare straight at a woman with red lipstick for seven seconds.

7. ***Good Posture***
   - In any life situation or condition, good posture always matters. Poor posture often leads to disrupted body image and different bone diseases. Most women who develop improper posture have low self-confidence and socialization problems. They are often shy and see themselves as unattractive and less-worthy. But remember ladies, you can always improve your posture by doing posture exercises and training. This will help you build that much-needed confidence to look more physically (and sexually) appealing to men.

8. ***Big Boobs***
   - Yeah, you heard it right! Big boobs are a thing in this journey of chasing the man of your dreams. Your cup size does matter.

Since men are highly sexual, they are easily drawn to women with big breasts. But the thing about boobies is often misunderstood by different groups of people. Some say having bigger breasts only encourages men to commit malicious thinking and sexual abuse to women. Men might stare longer at your breasts but that doesn't mean they will do something bad about you. Just understand the fact that it is a man's thing and what's important is their true intention. Remember, if you are confident about them, flaunt them!

9. ***Overall Grooming***
   - Overall grooming refers to the activities/routines that a person does to clean and maintain his body parts. A woman who is well-groomed and has good personal hygiene can be easily noticed by men. Personal grooming doesn't necessarily mean you have to apply heavy makeup and wear designer clothes. You just have to keep your body clean and presentable at all times. Good grooming also means being comfortable in your own body – regardless of your skin color, race, or appearance. When you accept everything about your body, men

will also accept you the way you are. Lastly, overall grooming can help you look younger and more alluring.

How to be More Attractive to Men

The truth is men don't only see the superficial beauty of a woman. They too, consider her personality and internal characteristics. Bear in mind that physical beauty is only a small part of being attractive. If you aren't blessed with superficial beauty, you can make use of your skills, talents, good characters, and innate abilities. As a woman, you need to learn how to accept you're your flaws or imperfections. This is necessary for you to live a life away from negativities and problems. That is the secret to genuine happiness. Always remember that you don't have to fully change yourself just for a man. If he doesn't like the way you look, just accept it and move forward. Then do everything to improve yourself and be a better woman someday.

How to Listen to a Guy

One of the less understood and often overlooked qualities of a woman is her ability to listen to a man. A woman who knows how to listen to a guy whenever he speaks is more likely to be appreciated by a guy. As a woman, you need to learn how to be an active listener. Never interrupt a guy when he is talking – especially when the topic matters a lot to him. Do not judge him about his opinions and undertakings on certain things in life. Let him know that you are willing to listen to his words. You can do this by simply nodding your head or giving verbal signs such as "Ok", "Yes", "That's right", etc. You can also paraphrase what he's said to let him know that you understand him. Do not tell him that his opinions are wrong and unfortunate. Guys need someone who will always listen to them no matter how hard the situation gets. Someone who will always support his opinions and not criticize him of his choices. A woman's listening ability may be always taken for granted, but this is probably the most important quality of a woman that men want in a girlfriend or wife. If you are a kind of woman who knows how to listen attentively to men, you are lucky!

5 Tips on How to be Confident around Men

To be confident around men, you first need to assess your level of self-confidence. You can check the level of your self-esteem by talking to yourself alone. This may sound weird, but this is the only way for you to prepare yourself and assure that you can do it. It is best to do it in front of the mirror.

While looking at your reflection in the mirror, examine your physical characteristics – your facial features, your body type, the length of your hair, etc. If you don't like what you see, you aren't that confident about the way you look. But if you're okay with it, you are on the right track. Then have some self-talk – ask yourself with different questions such as, "Am I really beautiful?", "Do I look good?", "Will a guy like me?", etc. After throwing yourself these questions, have some self-affirmation. Accept all these things about you and promise yourself that you are going to improve. Then finally, tell yourself "I will be more confident next time! I so can do it!"

After assessing your level of self-confidence, do the following:

1. *Be yourself.*
   - You don't need to wear a mask whenever you're talking to a guy. Learn the art of accepting your whole self – regardless of your imperfections and shortcomings. Never pretend to be someone you're not. Do not fear of being awkward during meetups. Men will like you when they know you are comfortable with your skin. Trust me, they will!

2. ***Be positive.***
   - Always be hopeful and positive. Remind yourself that you are special – someone who deserves all the love in the world. When things get rough, just look for the positive sides of the situation. Remember, all problems have a solution! Men choose a woman who remains cheerful and positive despite the uncertainties of the situation. They consider this woman as someone who can be a good partner in the future.

3. ***Take good care of your body.***
   - Your overall health and well-being are essential in keeping your goals intact and achievable. It is hard to be confident when you know you have a disease or compromised immunity. Do the typical ways of taking care of yourself - eating a well-balanced diet, exercising, and getting enough rest and sleep among others. Also, reduce stress to make your life even better. When you have a healthy mind and body, you will be more confident around men. Be always neat, clean, and presentable when you are dealing with men.

4. ***Show what you've got.***
   - Instill in your mind that you are not just a girl who wants to be recognized, but an extraordinary woman who deserves to be loved. You've got skills, talents, good character, and wonderful personality. Let the world know that you are a special being who can do better in life. Men will see that! Just remember, do this in the humblest way possible.
5. ***Learn how to flirt.***
   - This may sound controversial, but flirting, just like any other strategy, can also be a good way to attract men. The art of flirting can help women be more confident when dealing with men according to this study. The only problem with flirting is people associate it with sexual desires or intentions. But the truth is you can flirt without doing sex. Flirting simply means utilizing sexy techniques such as flipping hair to gain men's attention.

Confidence around men is a thing that can't be learned overnight. It takes time and constant practice before you master the art of being confident around men. For you to do it, take the first step. Start by having a self-affirmation - then everything else will follow. To help you build more confidence to deal with men efficiently, find a reliable support system. This can be your family, friends, members of the health industry, or women who have successfully overcome low-self-esteem. Just remember, do not overdo it!

Chapter 3 – Understanding the Surprising Truth about What Really Attracts Men

Men can be so mysterious and hard to understand. They love to keep things privately. It is difficult for men to express their true emotions and show their vulnerability. They always protect their ego and act as manly as they can be. Some men express their feelings in unconventional and hurtful ways. They do these to avoid rejections and failures. Men don't show their desire and passion easily. They wait until a woman explicitly allows them to show their overwhelming desire. As a woman, you need to understand the things that stimulate their interest. You also need to exert more time and effort in establishing a deep connection and emotional attachment with them. Men are attracted to a woman who devotes her time and energy to them. Making good connections with a man will help him open his heart and soul to you. He will also be more receptive to your suggestions and never be afraid of showing his vulnerability.

How to Build Deeper Connections with Men

According to American film producer and director Susan Johnson, for a couple to stay in the relationship, there should be a well-established emotional connection between them. Most women know exactly what they need for a healthy emotional connection – comfort, physical touch, deep conversation. However, connecting with a man on an emotional level can be challenging. You may have to exert a lot of effort and patience just to gain his trust and willingness to take the process. Remember, when building connections with a man, you have to give more focus on his needs. Although you will not benefit much from this, seeing your man opening his world for you can be so satisfying.

So how exactly can you build deep and genuine connections with men? Follow these tips:

1. ***Pay attention to what they say.***
   - Paying attention means listening attentively to their stories, rants, or advice. Men love it when a member of the opposite sex appreciates their opinions and life choices. While listening, observe their gestures, the tone of their voice, their emotions, and their expressions. Make sure you understand everything that they say. Do not interrupt them while they're talking. Also, provide an honest, immediate answer when they ask you a question.
2. ***Show respect.***
   - Respect is one of the major foundations of any kind of relationship. It is a form of a deep emotional connection that can be developed over time. It is necessary to

give men respect to show that you care. You can show them respect by considering and giving weight to their opinions. Another way is by avoiding sensitive topics that may potentially hurt them – especially those that affect their ego and self-esteem. Also, give them enough time and space to think.

3. *Show interest in his life.*
   - To create genuine connections with a man, take an interest in his life. Know his goals, ambitions, plans, etc. Be interested in his family background, career, achievements, and personal favorites. When you get to know him better, you are more likely to develop a bond that has the potential to last. One important thing to remember, do not ask questions about his previous love experiences during first meetings. That is completely a turnoff. He may think you are so into him and he might take advantage of you.

4. *Be mysterious.*
   - Being mysterious means, you don't need to not tell everything about your life during conversations with men. Your goal is for a man to pursue you. Do not feed him with so much information that he will only forget. When you share everything about your life, he will only get bored. If he is interested in you, he will devote his time and energy to know you better. Men

often pursue women who are less-talkative and mysterious.

5. ***Be intimate.***
   - Physical attraction can lead to something more intimate – like sex. The truth is you can also build an emotional connection with a man through sex. It is considered as the best love language that most people want. When a man trusts you, he considers you his own. He wants to own every inch of your body through sexual contact. When your bodies are united into one, you are sharing everything about you. Bear in mind that you have to be physically and emotionally ready before engaging in sexual activities with a man. If not, you can always utilize the power of touch, kisses, and hugs. Just remember, you can only have sex with a man if you have been consistently communicating or dating.

How to Make a Man Commit to You

Making men commit is probably one of the hardest things in the world. Men are naturally afraid of commitment and too much emotional attachment. This is because they don't want their freedom to be taken away easily from them. It takes an extremely valuable reason for a man to spend the rest of his life with you. Most men consider commitment as an important decision that they will be making in his lifetime. Make sure you have all the best reasons for a man to fall madly in love with you. If you want him to desperately want to commit to you, follow these tips:

1. ***Spend a lot of time with him.***
   - Your man will get to know you better if you spend most of your time with him. If possible, know all his activities and whereabouts for a day. Remind him of his daily schedule and wish him good luck. Some may think this can be irritating, but the truth is men appreciate it when there is somebody who seems to care about their life. Devoting your time with him is a sign of concern. If he gets used to it, he will constantly seek your presence. If your man can't live without your presence, he will pledge to make you his official girl and a lifetime partner.

2. ***Do not ask him about your status.***
   - Even though you have been officially dating for a long time, you still need to wait for his proposal. Never ask him about your role in his life or else, your world may shatter. Understand the fact that men are hesitant of committing with a woman and they need a valid reason for them to do that. Let him take control of this game of commitment and just follow his lead.

3. ***Let him miss you.***
    - Spare a day or two of not seeing each other. You can do this intentionally to know how long can he stand not having you by his side. Before you do this, make sure he is already drawn into you – or at least he's shown interest in you. If you think he likes you, then put him into this test. Just trust your woman's instinct. Men can also go crazy if they aren't able to see the love of their life even just for a day. And remember, absence makes the heart grow fonder.

4. ***Do not introduce him as your boyfriend.***
    - Every time you bring him to any gathering or meetup, introduce him as your friend. When you do this, he may think you aren't sure of your status and that you don't brag about him to your loved ones. Men want a woman who doesn't take the lead in the relationship. While introducing, observe his reaction. If he really likes you, he will get irritated and can be defensive about your real status. This will make him commit to you and ask you to be his official girl. And that's indeed a beautiful thing.

5. ***Do not push him to commit.***
    - This last tip is probably the most important among these five. Confronting your man about his true intentions is like destroying the castle that you built.

Forcing him to like you will only lead to disappointment and heartbreak. Men who take a longer time to commit may have commitment issues. You can't force them to commit easily. They have to do it on their own to overcome their fears.

Keeping Your Man Interested in You

When you see signs that a man is so into you, Congratulations! You are getting there. Now, the next thing to do is to keep him interested in you by doing things that can please him. Keep the momentum going, and never let it go. To help you keep your man interested in you forever, you may want to do the following:

- ✓ Appreciate the things he does.
- ✓ Always listen to him.
- ✓ Give him surprises and presents to let him know that you care.
- ✓ Boost his self-confidence and make him feel like a man.
- ✓ Show him that you're willing to wait.
- ✓ Match his level of commitment by doing extra efforts to keep the relationship going.
- ✓ Don't play hard to get.
- ✓ Never get jealous of his female friends. Remember, you are not his official lover.
- ✓ Do not be so clingy.
- ✓ Learn the right way of messaging or replying to his messages on social media platforms.

The Art of Replying to Your Man's Text Messages

Learning the art of replying to a man's messages can help build his interest in you. This will also keep him hooked and make him beg to see you again. When replying to a man's text message, follow these helpful tips:

- Avoid texting closed-ended questions or those answerable by Yes or No. Try texting him back using these open-questions, "How's your day?", "What do you exactly feel?", "How can I help you?".
- Do not send him "needy" messages such as, "I am not feeling okay.", "I hope you are here!", or "I need you right now."
- Text him something that will make him feel good such as "You're doing good!", "That's great!", or "You can do it!".
- Don't just say Hi or Hello. Try adding some extensions such as "Hi Mr. Gorgeous, hope everything's fine!" or "Hello there. Been thinking of you all night. Miss You! ☺"
- Text some comforting words such as "I am just here!", "I know you are strong, just keep the faith!", etc. -
- Use emojis or funny emoticons lightly. Do not use too many emoticons in just one message. That can be so annoying!

Chapter 4 – How to Charm a Guy and Make Him Want You as His Future Wife

Contrary to what you see on TV shows where men have the nerves (and balls) to approach women, men nowadays are more afraid of interacting with women. This is because they fear of being rejected by the woman they like. When a man sees an attractive woman, he tends to compare himself to other men who look better than him and have greater achievements in life. Whether we admit or not, the truth is women are most attracted to guys who possess alpha male characteristics. These include excellently good physique, lean muscles, nice facial features, etc. Women feel more secure and safe with a man who belongs to the Alpha male species. Less-attractive guys often feel insecure and shy towards women. They stay away from the woman they like and just wait for the right woman to come. A kind of woman who will accept him despite his imperfections and shortcomings.

How to Make a Man Approach You

When a man finds it hard to approach you, it is more likely that he lacks the courage to do the first move. You have to understand his situation and try to do ways to encourage them to get to know you. Here are the tips:

1. ***Smile at him.***
   - Your smile can mean a lot to him. That symbolizes a friendly behavior. Flashing your sweetest smile can also break the wall between the two of you – and that may be the start of a sweet romance.

2. ***Assure him that it's completely fine.***
   - A man may not approach you even though he is attracted to you because he lacks the confidence and the courage to do it. Let him feel accepted and assure him that it is okay to talk to you. Also, do not make yourself intimidating and overpowering. Possess a nice and friendly aura that will make him feel at ease around you.

3. ***Do not overdress.***
   - Wearing designer clothes can make you look more regal, classy, but intimidating. Men avoid women who are highly fashionable and are always dressed to kill. If you want men to approach you, wear simple, casual clothes. This will make you look more approachable and less intimidating.

4. ***Do not show him a high level of intelligence.***
   - It is a known fact that men prefer a woman who is intelligent and full of wisdom. However, having too much

"brain" can only result to not making a man get closer to you. An intelligent woman oftentimes sets a standard that can be hard to achieve. This can cause men to feel intimidated and less worthy. When talking to a man, do not tell him highly technical words and super hard questions that require Google-generated answers. In short, do not be a smart-ass!

5. *Have some manners.*

   - Having a good character is still the best weapon for you to win the battle of chasing Mr. Right. If you want a man to approach you, improve your character. Show him your good heart and your beautiful soul. Men give so much weight to a woman's behavior and personal manners. When they see a woman who possesses these traits, they won't let her go.

6. *Break the wall between you.*

   - Well, if you can't stand seeing him staring at you and just doing nothing, then make the first move! Break that wall that separates you from him. If he can't do it, then you do it! Greet him and start a mini conversation. When you know he's starting to be more at ease with your presence, slow down and let him do the talking. That could be the start of something good and special. Good Luck!

The Best Way to Charm a Guy

When a guy you like is been consistently seeing you, it is normal that you expect him to make you his better half. But sometimes, guys do not clearly state their true intention. They make things hard for you to understand. As a woman, you can only wait until he finally says, "Let's move this to another level." You can start up as friends to build a strong foundation for the "possible" relationship. While enjoying the friendship status you have with the guy, use your feminine charms. Make him go crazy over you and find you irresistible and alluring. But of course, in the right way! To make a man defenseless of your charm, be able to relate to him on a more personal level. Don't just use your physical attributes in attracting a guy. Instead, develop a higher level of intimacy with him – like deep personal connections. Refer to Chapter 3 for more info about building deeper connections with a man.

5 Things You Should Avoid Doing for a Man to Consider Your Relationship Marriage Worthy

When men commit on a relationship, they want it to last a lifetime. As a woman, you need to understand what men want and the things that can satisfy them. This is essential in building a solid foundation for your relationship. If you know the things that please your man can, he will learn to appreciate you more. Never do things that can ruin your relationship. The following are the things that you should avoid doing for him to consider your relationship a marriage-worthy one:

1. *Bragging*
   - Bragging about your achievements and resources to a man can only make him feel irritated and intimidated. Men are naturally egoistic and they don't like it when a woman is more superior to them. Even though you have more accomplishments in life than him, never boast about these things to your man. Just be humble and let him discover these things about you.
2. *Being Immature*
   - Men prefer a woman who is mature in dealing with life's situations. A kind of woman who can carry herself gracefully

and can stay positive during stressful times. Some women can easily get exhausted when faced with different problems in life. They oftentimes make bad decisions and aren't capable of handling life's circumstances. As a woman, you need to learn how to make good and wise decisions. You also need to be mature in handling different life situations and circumstances.

3. *Taking control of the relationship*
   - This is considered as one of man's innate characteristics. Our society views men as powerful leaders while women are just faithful followers. When you are seeing/dating a guy, just let him take control of the relationship. Be submissive but don't let him abuse you. As a woman, you are expected to always stay by his side and support his decisions. If you deeply wish to make him your future husband, learn to stay under his wings.

4. *Making him feel jealous*
   - Making your man feel jealous can lead to conflicts in the relationship. You need to assure him that he is the only man in your life and you aren't entertaining other men. When a man considers you his property,

he will do everything to keep you. Avoid doing things that will make him feel envious and unsure. If you remain faithful to him, he will make you his future life partner.

5. ***Invading his privacy***
    - Just like you, your man also needs privacy and some alone time to enjoy. Do not dare to invade his privacy if you want to make your relationship last. If he doesn't want to share his password on his social media accounts, respect his decision. If you trust him that much, you will let him enjoy his privacy. Women who respect their partner's privacy are more likely to find lifetime happiness with the man of their dreams.

Chapter 5 – Why Do Men Like a Woman Who is a Challenge

A challenging woman is someone who knows her self-worth or value. She does not easily give in to temptations and makes sure she protects her femininity at all times. Taming a powerful, challenging woman is like taking the hardest adventure of a lifetime. When a man pursues a challenging woman, he is really into her. He is more than willing to do everything just to win her. Men find a naturally challenging woman sexy and attractive. They see her as a special kind of woman who is real, genuine, and of high value. Being powerful does not mean you have to be in control of the dating game or relationship. As a woman, you are expected to do it naturally – without pretensions and dramas. You don't have to fake a thing. Do not act aloof or play hard to get just to get noticed. Men will notice if you are genuinely challenging or not. Remember, men are keen observers. They will certainly know if it's true or not.

Why Men Can't Resist a Naturally Challenging Woman

Here are the reasons why men like a woman who is a "challenge"

1. *Men naturally love to chase.*

   - Men are fun-and-adventure seekers. They love to do things that challenge their strength and manhood. This behavior may be associated with how men try to protect their ego and integrity. When a man sees an irresistible, challenging woman who makes them feel weak, they pursue her. Getting this woman gives them an extra dose of strength and self- confidence. Men know that a challenging woman is smart, sexy, and effort-worthy. They will do anything to get her no matter what the cost may be.

2. *Men are naturally competitive.*

   - Men love all kinds of competition. When the woman they like is surrounded by other men, they do everything to be the first to get her. Competition among men can be tough and physical. When men challenge other men to win the girl they all like, they take the challenge seriously. They know this girl is worth fighting for.

3. *A challenging woman is not more than just a sexual partner.*

   - When men are looking for a lifetime partner, they make sure she will be the one. They often choose a woman who is more than just a pretty face – a woman who has substance and worth. A woman who doesn't give in easily to temptations values her body and soul. She is a woman of integrity. Men often think that sex is the highest achievement they can get from pursuing a woman. But when sex becomes the only reason for a man to stay with a lady, he tends to get out of the relationship. Men want a definite and valid reason for them to stay committed to a woman. When they can't find any, they often quit the relationship. A naturally challenging woman can give a man enough reason to stay interested and committed to her. This is why men pursue this kind of woman.

4. *A challenging woman knows how to value the exclusivity of the relationship.*

- A challenging woman prefers a relationship that is exclusive and long-lasting. She takes dating seriously that's why she is patiently waiting for the right man to come along. A kind of man who will also take her seriously and will do everything to win her. A challenging woman may be hard to understand but the truth is, she is just afraid of showing what she truly feels. She gives so much value to the exclusivity of the relationship. This woman will do everything that she can to achieve this kind of relationship. Men understand that a woman who treats them hard is one that is worth pursuing. They know that this woman is faithful and loyal. A woman who can be a good wife someday.

5. *A naturally challenging woman values commitment.*

- Commitment is what makes a relationship last. A woman who values commitment is more likely to stay in the relationship for a long time (or until forever). Men prefer a woman who is naturally challenging because they know that this kind of woman knows how to commit. She also knows how to resist temptation which often leads to sexual interactions. A woman who knows how to commit looks for a deeper meaning of the relationship – not just sex alone. She makes sure a man is fully committed to her before giving her all self. She simply needs to be 100% sure before giving it a go.

How to Make a Man Fall Madly in Love with You

When you've finally met the man of your dreams, do everything to get him. Let him know your presence and know all the things that stimulate his interest. If you think this man will make you complete, don't dare let him go. To help you make him fall madly in love with, read these practical tips:

1. ***Never lose hope.***

    - Hope is what makes a person keep going. If you think that man is the one you've been praying for, trust yourself that he will be yours eventually. Do not lose hope and always stay positive. Just make sure you've already invested enough time and effort to that guy before considering him your potential lover. If not, be ready to accept the worst. Never lose hope. Remember, there are many fishes in the ocean. You will surely find a guy like him – or even more than him.

2. ***Improve your appearance.***

    - If you think your appearance makes you unattractive, do ways to improve it. People typically judge a person by the way he looks. Your best physical appearance will be your primary weapon to keep men hooked on you. That is what men first consider in searching for a woman. Always make yourself neat and presentable to men. You can wear makeup if that makes you feel good about yourself. But don't forget that men don't just consider the physical traits of a woman.

They look into more valuable things about you – your character, skills, and qualities.

3. ***Smile often.***

   - Your smile can change a man's mood. Make sure to flash your sweetest smile whenever your man is around. That will encourage him to get closer to you and make him start a conversation. When a man keeps seeing a woman who is always smiling, he is more likely to fall for her. Flashing your best smile to your man can also help ease his burdens in life. When he finally shares these with you, that could be the start of a deeper connection.

4. ***Make eye contact.***

   - Establishing a connection with your man can be done through making eye contact. This is essential in building rapport and trust. When your man is talking to you, gaze into his eyes, and let him know that you care. Assure him that his words are safe with you and he can fully trust you. You don't have to own a pair of blue eyes to make a man fall in love with you. Just look at him with sincerity and passion – that's all that matters.

5. *Make him feel special.*

- Treating him special will certainly make him want to know you better. A man who constantly receives attention from a woman considers that woman as a potential partner in life. To make him feel loved and adored, send him love messages through letters, texts, e-mails, etc. Give him gifts, food, or anything which will make him feel better. Soon he will realize that you are becoming a part of his life and he won't let you go.

6. *Accept him fully.*

- Accepting him for everything that he is will make a man more confident of himself. You don't have to change him because you know he needs to. If you really like him, just let him do the usual things he does. Remember, he has a life to live. He is not your property and you don't have the right (yet) to tell him what to do. If you find his style outdated and not appropriate, just keep it yourself. Do not interfere with his decisions and respect his choices. If you can't stand seeing him the way he is, then consider finding another guy who will pass your standards.

7. ***Bring out the best in him.***

- People have strengths and weaknesses in life. Those are what make them different from one another. If you focus on the negative characteristics of your man, you will never find happiness with him. If that guy shows his vulnerability to you, that means he trusts you. Make him feel confident of himself by encouraging him to never start trying. Focus on his strengths – his intellect, wisdom, productivity, etc. Teach him to believe in himself and that he can do greater things if he wants to.

How to Keep a Man Happy in a Relationship

To keep a man happy and content in the relationship, do these things:

- ✓ Understand him all the time but also remind him of his wrongdoings.

- ✓ Make him feel needed and loved.

- ✓ Talk to him often.

- ✓ Praise him for his achievements and good deeds.

- ✓ Let him take control of the relationship.

- ✓ Be always faithful to him.

✓ Tell him all the things that you do.

✓ Shower him with kisses and hugs.

✓ Satisfy his sexual needs.

✓ Most importantly, just love him no matter what.

If you do these things, your man will love and appreciate you more. When he is satisfied with the kind of love you are giving him, he won't ever consider cheating or leaving you. Keeping a man happy and content is the key to lifetime happiness. Good Luck!

Conclusion

Attracting the man of your dreams is never an easy task. You have to know and understand a man's behavior to make him fall for you. Since men are naturally mysterious and aren't vocal about their feelings, it is hard to know if they are attracted to you. Men need a lot of time to think about what they really want in life. They have to make sure of their feelings before sharing these with others. Since your main goal is to attract men, you have to pay attention to the things that build their interest. Learn about these things and use them to make them hooked into you.

Men don't show their desire and passion easily. They wait until a woman explicitly allows them to show their overwhelming desire. As a woman, you need to exert more time and effort in establishing a deep connection and emotional attachment with them. Men are attracted to a woman who devotes her time and energy to them. Making good connections with a man will help him open his heart and soul to you. He will also be more receptive to your suggestions and never be afraid of showing his vulnerability. A woman who is confident of herself is more likely to develop deeper connections with men.

Being confident around men can be challenging for some women. They are afraid to be judged by society. They also fear being labeled as a low-profiled woman who seeks attention from the opposite sex. Confidence around men is a thing that can't be learned overnight. It takes time and constant practice before you master the art of being confident around men. For you to do it, take the first step. Start by having a self-affirmation - then everything else will follow. While it's a known fact that men always look for the physical attractiveness of a lady, it is important to note that men also consider the totality of a woman. Most men are looking for a woman who is more than just a pretty face. A kind of woman who also possesses a good heart and soul. When a man finds the perfect woman for him, he is more than willing to commit to her.

When men commit to a relationship, they do everything to make it last a lifetime. Commitment is the key to keeping the relationship healthy and strong. To make your man commit in the relationship, show him that you are worthy of his love. Make him feel loved and special. Give him all the things that satisfy him.

As a woman, you need to understand what men want and the things that interest them. This is essential in building a solid foundation for your relationship. If you know the things that please your man can, he will learn to appreciate you more. Never do things that can ruin your relationship. Most importantly, remain honest and loyal to him all the time.

Another important quality of a woman that men find more attractive is her ability to listen to a man. As a woman, you need to learn how to be an active listener. Never interrupt a guy when he is talking – especially when the topic matters a lot to him. Do not judge him about his opinions and undertakings on certain things in life. Let him know that you are willing to listen to his words. Guys need someone who will always listen to them no matter how hard the situation gets. Someone who will always support his opinions and not criticize him of his choices.

This book can help women fully understand men in different aspects. What you have just read in this book will help you build deeper connections and meaningful relationships with different kinds of men. This will also help you be equipped with the necessary skills and knowledge for you take the dating game on a whole new level. You can use this book as a guide to maintaining a good relationship with the man you love. This will also help increase the levels of intimacy and commitment in your elationship. When a man gets a sufficient amount of attention and love from you, he will never cheat on you. He will forever love you and always make you feel special.

One important thing I want you to remember about this book is to always remain hopeful. Being alone does not necessarily mean you have to be depressed and hopeless. Always remember that there is hope in everything. Do not make your life miserable by making wrong choices and not embracing change. You can still improve your life and be the best person that you can be. You are special and you deserve all the love in the world because you are a woman. Always remember that!

Thank you so much for reading this book. What I want you to do next is to make all these things possible in your life. Use all these tips and techniques to find the man of your dreams. A kind of man who will be worthy of your love, time, and attention. The moment you find him, never let him go. Do all the things to keep him and never, ever let him go! Establish a deep connection with him and make him the center of your life. Also, make sure that he loves you so much and he is more than willing to stay with you until eternity.

Good luck!

-- [Daniel Monetier]

Check Out Other Books

Go here to check out other related books that might interest you:

The Ultimate Handbook to Exude Robust Confidence in 7 Days

https://www.amazon.com/dp/B07RJTCHKW

Unravel The Hidden Mystery Of What Women Want
In Men
http://www.amazon.com/dp/B07VBT265S

The Ultimate Procrastination Fix Handbook To
Achieve Your Goals and Increase Self Growth
http://www.amazon.com/dp/B07XTMDL5C